# PAINTING

## BEHIND THE SCENES

## ANDREW PEKARIK

HYPERION BOOKS FOR CHILDREN

NEW YORK

*i*

## SPECIAL THANKS:

I am very grateful to Alice Trillin and Jane Garmey for giving me the opportunity to participate in this project and for guiding me through it with enthusiasm, good ideas, and many kinds of practical assistance. I especially want to thank Kay Larson, who generously helped me at every stage of the work, sharing ideas, insights, and the joy of discovery.

First Edition

1 3 5 7 9 10 8 6 4 2

Library of Congress Cataloging-in-Publication Data

Pekarik, Andrew.
    Behind the scenes: painting /Andrew Pekarik — 1st ed.
        p.  cm.
    Summary: Discusses painting from an artist's viewpoint and uses specific examples to point out how to discover the details in a painting.
    ISBN 1-56282-296-9 (trade) — ISBN 1-56282-297-7 (lib. bdg.)
    1. Painting — Appreciation — Juvenile literature.  [1. Painting.
2. Art appreciation.]   I. Title.
ND1146.P45  1992
750′.1′1 — dc20   92-52987 CIP AC

**Behind the Scenes** is a production of Learning Designs, Inc., and WNET/THIRTEEN. Funders for the series include McDonald's Family Restaurants, the National Endowment for the Arts, the Corporation for Public Broadcasting, the Arthur Vining Davis Foundations, the John D. and Catherine T. MacArthur Foundation, the Andrew W. Mellon Foundation, the Bingham Trust, the Nathan Cummings Foundation, the Andy Warhol Foundation for the Visual Arts, and the George Gund Foundation.

# ACKNOWLEDGMENTS

Cover: *Camera and Chair* by David Hockney, 1986. © David Hockney.

Page 4: *The Loveletter* by Jan Vermeer, ca. 1669–70. Photograph courtesy of Rijksmuseum Foundation, Amsterdam.

Page 6: *The Bird Garden* by Paul Klee, 1924. Courtesy of Artothek, Staatsgalerie Moderner Kunst, Munich.

Page 8: *Number 30* by Ad Reinhardt, 1938. Private collection, on extended loan to The Whitney Museum of American Art, New York. Photograph by Bill Jacobson Studio, New York.

Page 11: *The Agony in the Garden* by Andrea Mantegna, ca. 1460s. Reproduced by courtesy of the Trustees, The National Gallery, London.

Page 15: *The Avenue, Middelharnis* by Meyndert Hobbema, 1689. Reproduced by courtesy of the Trustees, The National Gallery, London.

Page 16: *Tahmina Comes to Rustam's Chamber.* Artist unknown, ca. 15th century. Courtesy of The Arthur M. Sackler Museum, Harvard University, Cambridge, Massachusetts. Gift of Mrs. Elsie Cabot Forbes, Mrs. Eric Schroeder, and the Annie S. Coburn Fund.

Page 17: *Camera and Chair* by David Hockney, 1986. © David Hockney.

Page 18: *Three Musicians* by Pablo Picasso, 1921. Collection, The Museum of Modern Art, New York. Mrs. Simon Guggenheim Fund. Photograph © 1990 The Museum of Modern Art, New York.

Page 26: *Red Canna* by Georgia O'Keeffe, ca. 1923. Collection of the University of Arizona Museum of Art. Gift of Oliver James.

Page 28: *Painting Number 199* by Wassily Kandinsky, 1914. Collection, The Museum of Modern Art, New York. Nelson A. Rockefeller Fund (by exchange). Photograph © 1992 The Museum of Modern Art, New York.

Page 30: *The Scream:* Edvard Munch, 1893. © Oslo kommunes kunstsamlinger, Munch Museet.

Page 31: *Untitled* by Robert Gil de Montes, 1991. Courtesy Jan Baum Gallery. Photograph by Alan Barker.

Page 32: *Mother Combing Her Child's Hair* by Mary Cassatt, ca. 1901. Courtesy of The Brooklyn Museum. Bequest of Mary T. Cockcroft.

Page 36: *Aphrodite Teaching Eros How to Shoot.* Artist unknown, ca. 4th century B.C. Courtesy of Cliché des Musées Nationaux, Paris.

Page 38: *Reclining Nude in the Studio* by Henri Matisse, 1935. Courtesy of Mr. and Mrs. Nathan L. Halpern.

Page 40: *The Rock Near Montmajour* by Vincent van Gogh, 1888. Courtesy of Vincent van Gogh Foundation, Vincent van Gogh Museum, Amsterdam.

Page 42: *Portrait of Joseph Roulin* by Vincent van Gogh, 1889. Collection, The Museum of Modern Art, New York. Gift of Mr. and Mrs. A. M. Burden, Mr. and Mrs. Paul Rosenberg, Nelson A. Rockefeller, Mr. and Mrs. Armand Bartos, Sidney and Harriet Janis, Mr. and Mrs. Werner E. Josten, and Loula D. Lasker Bequest (by exchange).

Page 43: *Ice Cream Cone* by Wayne Thiebaud, 1991. Private Collection. Courtesy Alan Stone Gallery. Photograph by Alan Barker.

Page 44: *Woods and Valleys of Mount Yü* by Ni Tsan, 1372. Courtesy of the Metropolitan Museum of Art, Gift of The Dillon Fund, 1973 (1973.120.8).

Page 47: *Number 32, 1950* by Jackson Pollock, 1950. Courtesy of The Kunstsammlung Nordrhein-Westfalen, Düsseldorf. © 1992 The Pollock-Krasner Foundation/ARS, New York.

Page 50: *Don Manuel Osorio Manrique de Zuñiga* by Francisco Goya, ca. 1784–92. Courtesy of The Metropolitan Museum of Art, The Jules Bache Collection, 1949 (49.7.41).

Page 52: *The Fortune Teller* by Georges de La Tour, ca. 1632–35. Courtesy of The Metropolitan Museum of Art, Rogers Fund, 1960 (60.30).

Page 54: *Playing the Ch'in Under Pine Trees* by Kano Motonobu, ca. 16th century. Courtesy of The Mary and Jackson Burke Foundation. Photograph by Rudolf Nagel.

Page 56: *Harriet Tubman Series No. 9* by Jacob Lawrence, 1939–40. Courtesy of Hampton University Museum, Hampton, Virginia.

Page 57: *Harriet Tubman Series No. 10* by Jacob Lawrence, 1939–40. Courtesy of Hampton University Museum, Hampton, Virginia.

Page 58: *Rooms by the Sea* by Edward Hopper, 1951. Courtesy of Yale University Art Gallery. Bequest of Stephen Carlton Clark.

# TABLE OF CONTENTS

# INTRODUCTION

This book is about how to look at and think about paintings and drawings. Looking at art is not the same as looking and seeing in everyday life. It is more like being a detective. One begins by searching carefully for the small clues that eventually break open the case. In this book you will get practice in discovering the details that most people miss.

You will also get practice in thinking like an artist. Artists are trained to think of their work using ideas such as *perspective*, *color*, *line*, and *composition*. These are four key concepts that underlie all great paintings. Once you learn how to recognize them, you'll begin to notice them more in other paintings. As you develop your looking skills and your ability to think like an artist, you will find that art is like a new language that can lead you to interesting ideas and feelings.

One more thing: This book uses photographs of paintings and drawings. Looking at a photograph of a painting is a very different experience from looking at an actual painting. For example, some of the paintings that are reproduced in this book are in actuality very large, so you would be surprised if you saw them in person. If you want to visit them, look up their locations in the list on page iii. You might also want to stop by your local museum and see if it has other works by the same artists in its collection. Looking at art is most fun when it is done in person.

# FLAT AND DEEP

Artists usually paint on flat surfaces, such as canvas or wood, but when you look at their paintings you often feel that you are looking into space. You can think about any painting in these two ways—as a flat surface with paint on it or as an imaginary space.

When you think of the painting as a flat object with a crust of paint on it (like a floor with something spilled on it), you will concentrate on the shapes of the paint areas, their colors and textures, and the ways in which they relate to one another.

If you think of the painting as an imaginary space (like a window), you will notice that some paintings appear to be shallow, whereas others look deep and seem to extend far into the distance. Artists can manipulate the sense of space in their paintings by using special techniques and systems of perspective.

This chapter introduces deep paintings, shallow paintings, and flat paintings; explains some of the techniques artists can use to create a sense of space in paintings; and shows how some artists combine flat and deep in the same painting.

# DEEP

On the flat surface of the canvas of *The Loveletter* the artist Jan Vermeer painted an imaginary space that you can picture walking into. This deep space seems to contain two rooms. Closest to you is a dark room that has a chair on the right, a curtain overhead, and a map on the left-hand wall. Beyond the dark room is a brightly lit room with black and white floor tiles, a fireplace, and paintings on the wall.

Because the dark room encloses the bright room, you feel as if you are standing in the dark one looking into the bright one. By dividing the painting into two deep rooms, the artist seems to put a distance between you and the woman in

**The Loveletter,** Jan Vermeer, ca. 1669–70
Oil on canvas, 17 3/8" x 15 1/8"

4

yellow. In the middle of her music practice she is interrupted by her servant, who brings her a love letter. The woman seems startled. She looks over as if to ask, "Who is it from?" Are you too far away to hear? The two women don't see you. Do you feel as if you are secretly watching? The depth of the painting creates suspense. When the woman turns her head back, will she see you?

To see how the artist used tricks to make the painting look deep, try this experiment. Take four pieces of white paper and lay them on the picture, one on each side of the bright room, so that you cover all of the dark room, including the curtain at the top and the broom at the bottom. Do you see how shallow the remaining space has become? The woman now seems closer. Does she also seem less interesting?

**The Bird Garden,** Paul Klee, 1924
Watercolor on paper, 10 1/2" x 15 3/8"

In Paul Klee's painting red birds and white birds sit in a garden. How deep is the space in this garden? Can you imagine walking into it? Which birds are in the front of the space and which are in back? How can you tell?

The birds seem to represent two different types, with the red ones larger than the white ones. They are all quiet birds–their mouths are shut. Because their wings are closed, they must be standing instead of flying. But what are they standing on? One white bird and one red bird are upside down. How is that possible? What do you think the rectangular shapes represent? Plots of ground? Fences? Baskets?

All the birds are shown in profile, as if they were sitting for their portraits. They look very flat. Even the leaves of the plants seem pasted on to the surface, like cardboard cutouts that you might make to form the backdrop for a puppet show. The painting gives you the idea of a garden with birds, and if you work at it you can imagine a very shallow space. But the painting does not encourage you to mentally move into it, and there is no feeling of suspense, as there is in the painting by Vermeer.

Everything is right up front and out in the open. "Here it is," the artist says, "the bird garden." It seems cheerful, simple, and obvious–the kind of painting a child might do. But when you look more closely you start to wonder. Why are two birds upside down? What are those rectangular shapes? Why was the painting made on newspaper whose print is still visible through the brown pigment?

# FLAT

**Number 30,** Ad Reinhardt, 1938
Oil on canvas, 40 1/2" x 42 1/2"

This painting by Ad Reinhardt is a lively arrangement of colors and shapes that look completely flat. It is very hard to imagine any space inside it. The painting seems to be just a lot of colors that bump and vibrate against one another, but it holds some secrets for those who look at it carefully.

Because the painting is so flat, you will probably first notice the shapes of the color areas. Almost all of the shapes are made with straight lines, although they are not rectangles because their sides do not meet in right angles. There is, however, one complete circle and one semicircle in the painting. Can you find them?

Reinhardt composed this painting with great care. He believed that order and geometry underlie the confusion of things in the world. He wanted to simplify everything that goes on inside his picture so that its essential parts would be clear to the viewer. The straight lines help the picture stay in balance. The patches of color are so evenly painted that they look like cutout pieces of colored paper.

If you imagine the painting as an arrangement of cut-out paper pieces, you will notice new connections between the patches of color. For example, around the edge of the whole picture is a border of solid bluish gray.

Now that you have been looking at this picture carefully for a while, have you noticed the three special colors? Each one is used only once, while all the other colors are used many times. (They are pink, yellow-orange, and yellow.)

The longer you look at this picture, the more connections you will see between the colors and shapes. How do they fit together? Are they confusing or just complex? Are they quiet, or are they boring? Would you call them active? Wild? Would you agree that they express feelings that words cannot exactly describe?

# FOUR WAYS TO MAKE PAINTINGS LOOK DEEP

Jesus is on his knees, praying and looking at the angels in the sky. Three apostles, tired of waiting, have fallen asleep. In the distance, Judas, the apostle who betrayed Jesus, points the way for the soldiers who will take Jesus away to imprison and later crucify him. Jesus lived in Palestine, but the artist Andrea Mantegna lived in a city called Mantua, in Italy, and he made the city in the picture look like his own town, with castlelike towers and huge walls. Artists frequently use their own surroundings as the settings for famous events of the past.

The placement of the figures within the painting adds to the drama and suspense of the scene. In this painting, Mantegna uses the techniques of *size, overlap, groundline,* and *foreshortening* to suggest the deep space in which the event occurs.

**The Agony in the Garden,** Andrea Mantegna, ca. 1460s
Oil on wood, 24 1/2" x 31 1/5"

**SIZE:** Mantegna drew the soldiers much smaller than Jesus or his apostles so they would look farther away. The soldiers get smaller and smaller until the ones in front of the city gate are hardly more than tiny dots. In real life, objects of the same size look smaller when they are farther away, so painters can use size to give a sense of depth to the space in their paintings.

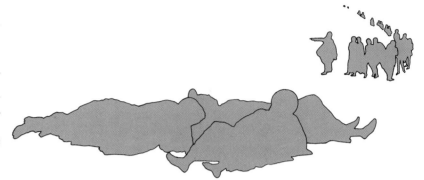

**GROUNDLINE:** If you can see the ground between two objects, you have a sense of how far apart they are. Because you can trace most of the road between Jesus and the soldiers, you can imagine how long it will take them to arrive. This feeling of distance and time helps to build suspense and tell the story.

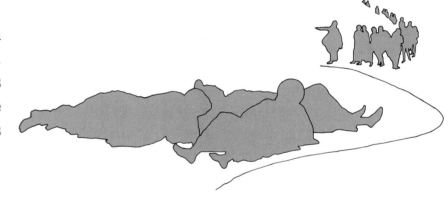

**OVERLAP:** When something is in front of something else, it covers over part of the thing behind it. The apostle in pink, for example, covers up, or overlaps, part of the apostle in red and green, so he must be the one in front. Using overlap makes the space inside the painting look bigger because it has to hold all of the overlapping objects, one in front of another.

**FORESHORTENING:** Of the three sleeping apostles in front of the rock, the two closest to the rock are lined up head to head from right to left. Because you are looking at them from the side, you can see their whole shapes. They are about the same height (try measuring them with a ruler, head to toe). But because the sleeping apostle on the right (holding the book) is pointing toward you with his feet, you cannot see his whole shape. Measure him with your ruler and you will find that his shape is squashed, or foreshortened. When you see a figure or an object that has been foreshortened, such as the sleeping apostle on the right, you naturally feel that the painting is deep because it has enough space to hold the figure lying diagonally in the scene. By putting this foreshortened figure right in the front of the scene, the artist wanted to draw us immediately into the imaginary space of the painting so that we would become involved in the drama.

Jesus knows that he is going to die, and you can see the soldiers coming, but his friends the apostles are sound asleep on the wrong side of the rock. They won't know trouble is coming until it is too late. You wonder how long it will take the soldiers to arrive. You want to tell the apostles to wake up, but you cannot. The world the artist has invented inside the painting looks very real, but it is not. The soldiers will never move. The suspense will never end.

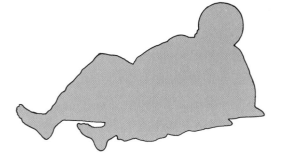

# A REALISTIC PERSPECTIVE SYSTEM

Over thousands of years and in regions throughout the world, artists have used many different ways of suggesting space on the flat surfaces of their paintings. One of these methods was developed in Europe in the fifteenth and sixteenth centuries. This particular system arose from careful, scientific study of the way we actually see things. One of the rules is that if you represent a road going into the distance, the two sides of the road will meet at a point on the horizon. Paintings made according to this perspective system look very realistic.

When you look at a picture drawn in a realistic perspective system, you feel as if you are looking through a window. But the view through a window changes if the things you see through it move or if you move. Try this with a real window to see what I mean. In order for the picture to stay the same, your eye, the frame, and the subject have to stay in exactly the same place without moving. When a painting is made in a completely convincing perspective, you seem to be standing at precisely one point, just as if you were looking through a real window.

When you look at Meyndert Hobbema's painting, you find yourself in the middle of the road, and you feel that you cannot move from that one spot. Try an experiment: Put this book flat on a table and move your head down

**The Avenue, Middelharnis,** Meyndert Hobbema, 1689
Oil on canvas, 40 1/3" x 55"

toward the table on either the right or left side of the book. You will notice that no matter from what angle you look at this picture, it still seems as if you are standing in the middle of that road.

The sense of being in precisely one place as you look at a painting can create strong feelings. In the painting by Vermeer, for example, you may feel curious about the woman and the letter, but it is hard to imagine entering the room. In the Mantegna painting, you want to tell the apostles to wake up, but you feel that you cannot because you are stuck in one place by the artist's own perspective system. And in Hobbema's work you are forced to stay on the road. Wouldn't it be interesting to take the road to the right and visit the houses? Or, even better, to take the small path to the left and explore the dark grove of woods?

# MULTIPLE POINTS OF VIEW

Many artists use perspective systems that do not put you in exactly one spot. These artists are not trying to make their paintings look as much like the real world as possible. They are more interested in other ideas.

This painting from west Asia is part of a story about the kings of Persia. The shy Tahmina has just married the noble Rustam, and a slave has guided her to Rustam's room, where the lovers will spend their first night together. The scene does not look completely realistic because this perspective system uses more than one point of view at the same time.

Where are you watching this scene from? At first it seems as if you are high off the floor, probably in an upper window in one of the walls of the room. But look at the rug under Rustam's bed. It is shown as if you were looking straight at it, as if it were pasted to the opposite wall. If that were the case, poor Rustam would slide right off it. What's going on here?

This artist followed the principle of showing a different point of view for each item in the painting. He wanted to present each thing from the angle where he thought it

**Tahmina Comes to Rustam's Chamber,**
artist unknown, ca. 1434–40
Opaque watercolor, ink, and gold on paper, 8 1/4" x 4 1/2"

looked best. The beautiful design on the rug under Rustam's bed looks best if you see it from directly overhead, so the artist moved our vantage point there for the rug. But Rustam looks better if you see him from the side, so the artist switched our viewing position for Rustam and his bed.

If you study this painting carefully you will see that there is one viewing position for the vases and another for the table they sit on. There is one viewing position for the wall and another for the floor. What is the best viewing position for Tahmina?

---

In the painting on the right the British artist David Hockney didn't care which view of a chair looks best. He assumed you already know how a chair actually looks from any fixed spot. He wanted this painting to remind you that your view of a chair changes as you move around it. There is not one perfect view of a chair, but many, many views. Almost every time you look at a chair, you see it differently. Your mind somehow puts all these views together. Hockney wants you to be aware that your ideas about the chair come from your memories of walking around it, so he gives you many viewpoints, all happening at once. Because we stand still when we look at his painting, doesn't it seem that the chair is moving and twisting?

**Camera and Chair,** David Hockney, 1986
Pastel on paper, 40" x 60"

17

# BOTH FLAT AND DEEP

In the twentieth century some artists have been fascinated by the realization that a painting could be thought of as both a flat surface and a deep space. They created paintings that make you think both ways at the same time.

**Three Musicians,** Pablo Picasso, 1921
Oil on canvas, 79" x 87 3/4"

Pablo Picasso's painting, like Vermeer's, has space and a story, but its real importance comes from the way it turns flat, geometric color shapes into a bold new form. Picasso was very talented and painted in many styles, including traditional perspective, but he also liked to explore new types of painting. He and his friend Georges Braque invented cubism, the style he used in this painting. Cubism is a kind of coded visual language, a language that Picasso is playing with in *Three Musicians*. He simplified a picture into its basic parts and rearranged the color shapes into a vibrant composition. The shapes are obviously flat, but they tell a story in a way that seems to place the characters in a strange, shallow room, a cubist space—mostly flat, but slightly deep—that is an invention of the twentieth century.

Clues in the painting tell us what is happening. The easiest clues to find are the eyes and noses at the top. They tell us that this is a painting of three people. You can see their feet at the bottom of the picture. They wear odd costumes. The recorder player on the left has a tall hat, the guitar player in the center is dressed like a clown, and the singer on the right has a hood like a monk's (and bare feet, too, because there are hints of his toes).

There is depth in this painting, although not very much. The guitar player overlaps both of the other figures. On the left and right sides of the painting we see the groundline where the floor meets the walls. The brown shape in front of the recorder player looks as if it might be a table, and the guitar player seems to be resting his right arm on it, but table legs are hard to find. The monk has music sitting on his lap. He is the singer. (His mouth is open.)

There are many more elements in this painting. Can you find the hands? The dog? They do not appear in exactly the place, shape, or size we would expect in real life.

Reinhardt used color shapes to set up a kind of rhythm. Vermeer's deep space created suspense. Picasso used both flat color and shallow space to present the drama of this musical event. The musicians are strange and unreal, like creatures from a new world. Their angles and edges merge perfectly with their geometric surroundings. You seem to be standing right in front of them in this small room.

This is a private concert for you. What kind of music do you hear? Is it anything like the colors?

# COLOR

Color is one of the first things you notice when you look at a painting, but unless the color is unusual in some way, like a green sky or a purple dog, you probably do not think about it very much. Because color is everywhere, it is easy to take for granted.

Painters are color experts. They need to know how to mix colors, how people respond to colors, how colors can represent feelings, and how to use colors to help tell a story.

If you think about color the way an artist does, you can make more interesting paintings of your own. This awareness will also help you to better understand the ideas and feelings that artists reveal to you in their paintings.

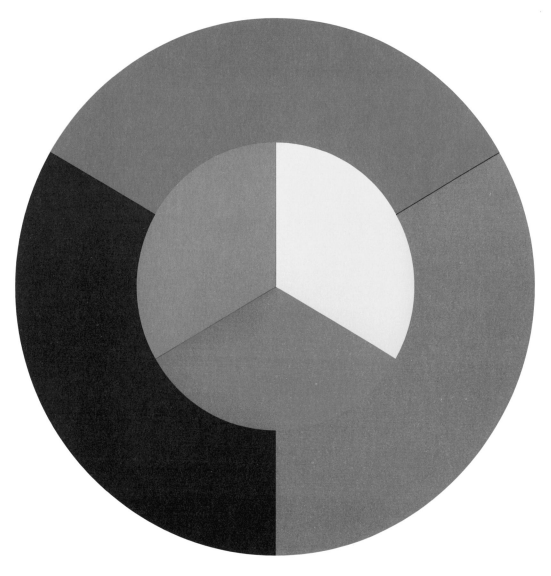

# MAKING COLOR

All colors except white and black can be made by mixing together different proportions of three basic colors: cyan, magenta, and yellow. These three colors are at the center of the color mixing wheel shown here.

If you mix magenta and yellow, you get red. Yellow and cyan make green, and cyan and magenta make dark blue. These mixtures are shown on the first ring of the wheel out from the center. As you keep adding some cyan or magenta or yellow to previous mixtures, you create more and more colors. This wheel shows only a small fraction of the total possibilities.

Colors that are near one another on the color wheel are like relatives—they have a lot in common. Colors that are opposite one another on the color wheel have the least in common and are called complementary colors.

Green and magenta are complementary colors because green is made by mixing cyan and yellow, placing it directly opposite magenta on the wheel. This distance from each other on the color wheel means that they have nothing in common. If the two complementary colors are mixed together, they produce a neutral tone—gray.

Cyan and red are also complementary colors. So are yellow and dark blue. Complementary colors make strong contrasts when they appear side by side. If you mix all the colors together, you get a dark brown, almost black.

Mixing painting colors is very different from mixing light, because paint and light work in different ways. Light looks white if it *contains* all of the colors in it. But paint looks white if it absorbs none of these light colors and *reflects* all of them. Red light is white light with all the colors except red filtered out, but red paint is paint that absorbs all the colors of white light *except* red.

# COLOR AND PERCEPTION

Your mind and eye influence the colors you see. Try the following experiments:

### EXPERIMENT 1:

The way a color looks depends on the color next to it. Do you agree that the intersecting lines at the top are darker than the intersecting lines at the bottom? It certainly looks that way. But they are not. To prove this, take two pieces of white paper and put one to the right of the vertical line and one to the left of it so that you cannot see the yellow or the violet The line is exactly the same color all the way from top to bottom. But when you see the intersecting lines next to a darker color on the bottom they look lighter, and when you see them next to a lighter color on the top they look darker. Artists must think about each color they use because each one influences the way the others are seen.

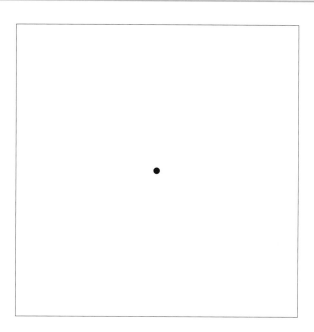

## EXPERIMENT 2:

The way your eye works influences the colors you see. Stare at the black dot in the middle of the red star for thirty seconds. Count to make sure, because you have to concentrate to keep your eyes steady on the dot for such a long period. Then quickly look at the black dot in the middle of the white space to the right of the red star. You will see the same star, but this time it is green.

Why does this happen? One theory is that when you look at the color red steadily for a long time, it tires out the rods and cones (the light-sensitive receptors) in the retina of your eye that are tuned to receive red. When you switch suddenly to the white space your eye does not respond to the red light that is being reflected off the white paper, so you see only the other reflected wavelengths in white light, which form the complementary color of red, namely, green. As the tired-out rods and cones recover, the afterimage disappears.

All of the pictures in this book are printed using this concept. If you look at any of these pictures with a microscope, you will see that the many different colors are all composed of tiny dots in the three basic colors: cyan, magenta, and yellow.

# COLOR HARMONY AND CONTRAST

Colors that are close to one another on the color wheel harmonize well, and those on opposite sides of the color wheel contrast strongly.

**Red Canna,** Georgia O'Keeffe, ca. 1923
Oil on canvas mounted on Masonite, 36" x 29 7/8"

This painting by Georgia O'Keeffe is inspired by a flower called a canna lily. The principal color is red, used in different intensities ranging from a rich dark red to a light pink. To add contrasting colors the artist went in one direction around the color wheel to orange and yellow, and also in the opposite direction to a light purple or lavender.

Within the range of colors O'Keeffe has chosen, yellow and lavender are at the extreme ends. They are nearly complementary to one another and make an intense color contrast. But all of these colors are located in a little more than half of the color wheel, opposite the greens and blues.

Examine this painting as if it were a conversation between two strong-willed colors. Take a sheet of paper and block off the upper half of the painting. Notice how yellow and lavender are positioned in the lower half. Yellow appears symmetrically on the right and left near the bottom. Moving up, lavender appears on the right and left but closer to the center. Exactly at the center is a bright tongue of yellow.

Move the paper to cover the bottom half of the painting. Yellow and lavender have now touched at the center, and both swell upward toward the top. A bit of yellow and lavender appear on the right side, too, but the colors stay apart from one another, as though unfriendly. You have probably noticed how surprising the little sliver of white seems near the top. The color in the painting is so carefully controlled that a spot without color is unusually powerful.

This fascinating painting suggests many things besides the canna flower of its title—one way of enjoying it is to follow the story of yellow and lavender meeting in the red center and spreading the energy of their argument upward.

**Painting Number 199,** Wassily Kandinsky, 1914
Oil on canvas, 64 1/8" x 48 3/8"

# COLOR AS SUBJECT

Almost all the different colors of the color wheel on page 22 are somewhere in the painting by Wassily Kandinsky. Some of them are just one or two strokes of the brush; others are larger patches. The longer you look, the more colors you can find.

But what is the painting about? None of the shapes and colors suggest familiar objects, as they do in Picasso's and O'Keeffe's paintings, and none of them are abstract colored blocks, as in Reinhardt's painting. They create an amazing feeling of turmoil, however. All the colors and shapes seem to be twisting and moving in unpredictable ways.

The two main colors in this painting are yellow and black. Kandinsky associated colors with emotions. Kandinsky felt that yellow "strained toward the spectator" and was like "human energy which attacks every obstacle blindly and goes forth aimlessly in all directions." He said that black "is something burnt out, like the ashes of a funeral pyre, something motionless like a corpse. The silence of black is the silence of death."

You can imagine this painting, then, as the struggle between yellow optimism and black death. The other colors add their unique accents to this epic battle.

Kandinsky linked colors with spiritual ideas and music as well as with emotions. According to Kandinsky, the ultimate feeling that blue creates is one of rest. "As it grows lighter it becomes more indifferent. In music a light blue is like a flute, a darker blue a cello; a still darker the marvelous double bass; and the darkest blue of all—an organ."

Green was also a restful color for Kandinsky: "In music, absolute green is represented by the placid middle notes of a violin." Light warm red, he said, "gives a feeling of strength, vigor, determination, triumph. In music, it is a sound of trumpets, strong, harsh and ringing." Not all artists would agree with him. What do *you* think?

Now you can see why there are no familiar shapes in this painting and why it seems so full of motion. Kandinsky is trying to paint a visual equivalent of life and death, music and silence, excitement and rest. The ideas he is trying to communicate are too large for ordinary images and too complex for words.

**The Scream,** Edvard Munch, 1893
Tempera and casein on cardboard, 36" x 29"

Color can have a powerful, direct effect on the way you feel. Some painters deliberately enlist the emotional force of color.

The Norwegian artist Edvard Munch created this haunting image in response to an actual event that he described in his diary:

*I was out walking with two friends—the sun began to set—suddenly the sky turned blood-red—I paused, feeling exhausted, and leaned on a fence—there was blood and tongues of fire above the blue-black fjord and the city—my friends walked on, and there I stood, trembling with fear—and I sensed an endless scream passing through Nature.*

Munch has tried to re-create the intense, mad red color that triggered his experience of a scream. The fjord, with two boats, is blue, and the shoreline is brown and green. Farther down the walkway are two friends.

Line has also been used to tell the story. The brown lines of the walkway (which was made by man) are straight and orderly, but the colorful lines of nature (red, yellow, blue, and green) swirl crazily as if illustrating the scream. Which world does the vacant-eyed man belong to? The world of man or the world of nature?

The painting by the contemporary artist Robert Gil de Montes also uses color and light to help make an emotional point. A blue-faced man with wings floats upward alongside smoke rings from a seashore, which is also a stage. A setting (or rising) sun highlights his left side. The red ground seems too hot to touch, and the man rises into light blue and cool green. Imagine how different the painting would be if the ground were green and the curtain red.

What's going on here? Why are there spooky eyes on the man's wings? Is this man supposed to be the artist? Does he feel like he's always onstage, being stared at by everyone? Is he trying to get away? Is this a dream? If so, is it a happy dream or a nightmare?

**Untitled,** Robert Gil de Montes, 1991
Oil on canvas, 40" x 60"

# COLOR AND EMOTION

**Mother Combing Her Child's Hair,** Mary Cassatt, ca.1901
Pastel and gouache on tan paper, 24" x 33"

# COLORS HELP TELL A STORY

In the peaceful scene depicted in Mary Cassatt's drawing, the little girl's hair is being combed by her mother. Neither the girl nor her mother is speaking. This tender, affectionate moment is described by the soothing curves of the figures and by the gentle colors. The girl's white dress catches your eye right away.

Cassatt, an American, lived in Paris and was a friend and colleague of some of the impressionist painters. The impressionists believed that a painting should capture a passing moment the way the eye actually sees it. Cassatt has framed the mother and daughter inside the lines of the green trim on the chair in which the mother sits. Another green border, framing a mirror on the wall, defines the reflected scene. These two green frames enclose two aspects of the same event.

Compare the central view with the reflected view. The colors look darker in the mirror image (especially the hair colors). Why is this? Where is the window in the room? How does that affect the colors?

More remarkable, the mother's expression seems to change. In the chair, where the colors of her face are bright, she seems to be concentrating on her combing while the girl stares dreamily. In the mirror, where she is darker, she seems to be thinking about the girl, mentally talking to her. There are two kinds of wordless exchange taking place in the drawing, two worlds distinguished by light and color. In the chair, the physical touch between mother and daughter is emphasized, but in the world of the mirror, it is the interplay of their thoughts that comes alive.

# LINe

Lines are basic elements in painting and drawing, partly because of the way the most common drawing tools work. Pencils, pens, crayons, brushes, sticks, and fingers all make lines naturally.

Artists often use lines to represent objects in simplified form. When you first started to draw, you probably sketched a house by drawing a triangle on top of a square. Anyone who looked at that drawing knew immediately that those lines stood for a house because they formed the outline of a typical house shape. In the course of everyday life you have learned the typical shapes of thousands of things. An artist just has to draw a simple outline to represent one of them.

A line can also be interesting by itself. Some lines seem fat and slow, others sleek and fast, others confused and nervous. Artists can use such lines to communicate feelings and moods, from energy and excitement to relaxation and calm. In many paintings and drawings lines are both descriptive and expressive at the same time. They not only represent something you recognize but also communicate feeling and emotion just by the way they are drawn.

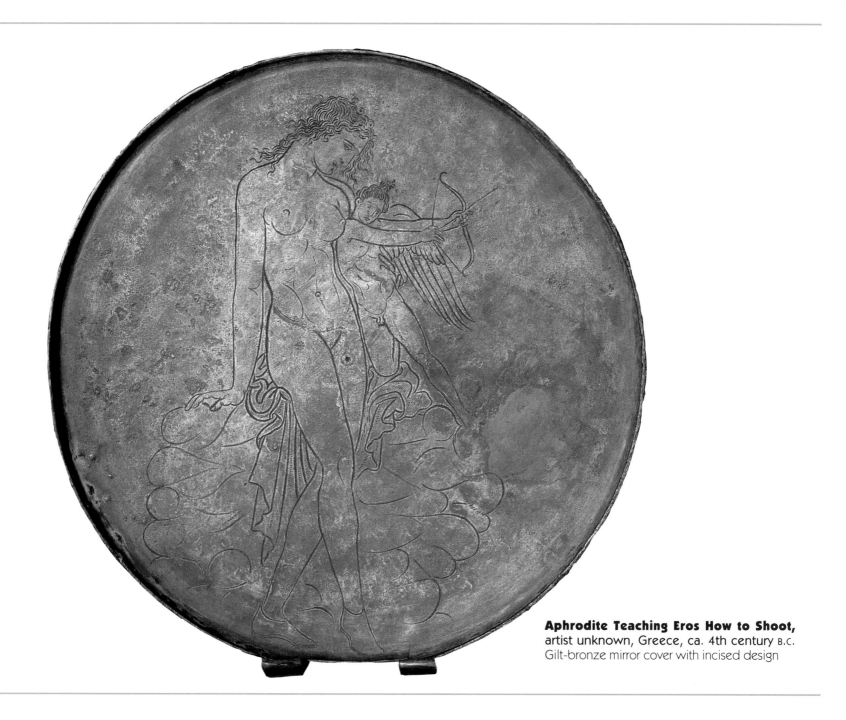

**Aphrodite Teaching Eros How to Shoot,**
artist unknown, Greece, ca. 4th century B.C.
Gilt-bronze mirror cover with incised design

# OUTLINE

The inside of this round metal mirror cover (used to protect the shiny surface of a metal mirror from getting scratched) was made in ancient Greece about twenty-three hundred years ago. The drawing was carved into the metal with a sharp-pointed tool.

Standing in the center is Aphrodite, the Greek goddess of love and beauty. The artist represented her with just a simple outline and a few details. You can see from her shape that she is a lovely goddess, with perfect proportions. But the artist's line is so skillful that you can also sense how her weight is balanced, how she supports herself with her right hand and leans back against some object that is partly draped with cloth.

Aphrodite's left arm is around Eros, the Greek god of love (the ancient Romans called him Cupid). She is teaching him how to shoot an arrow. Notice the narrow space between the line that forms the edge of Aphrodite's body and the line that forms the edge of Eros's body. That tiny gap tells you that Eros is holding himself in the air with his wings.

But what is Aphrodite leaning against? Is it a rock? A giant seashell? A wall? A cloud? Outlines describe things only if we recognize the shapes they make. This shape is hard to understand (maybe the artist didn't have anything specific in mind), but it probably represents something unpleasantly hard or cold, because the artist gave Aphrodite the cloth to lean on and also put shoes on her feet. What do you think it is?

**Reclining Nude in the Studio,** Henri Matisse, 1935
Pen and ink on paper, 17 3/4" x 22 3/8"

# EXPRESSIVE OUTLINE

Henri Matisse made this drawing with the thin, even ink lines of his pen. In the center you can recognize the relaxed form of a woman lying on a carpet. She is drawn in outline, like Aphrodite on the Greek mirror cover, but the line only suggests the shape of the woman. Notice her toes, for example, or the odd shape of her right hand. The wandering pen implies her contours without having to copy them exactly.

A drawing reproduces what the artist sees or imagines, but first the image is filtered through the artist's mind, feelings, and hand. The tool the artist chooses (perhaps a pen or pencil or brush dipped in ink) leaves its own special mark. Matisse's lines are very personal. If another artist sat in the same spot Matisse did and drew the same woman, the drawing might be completely different.

As you explore the rest of the picture you will find that the same woman appears two more times. She shows up in a mirror reflection in the top-left corner and also on a piece of paper in the lower-right-hand corner—where we see Matisse's right hand and pen making this drawing.

The woman's outline in the mirror is looser than the direct view of her in the center, but the woman in the drawing on the lower right is the sketchiest of them all. Matisse seems to be making a small joke about art. He seems to be asking, If the mirror image is more exact than the image drawn by an artist, why should the artist try to imitate a mirror? Why not relax and draw like an artist?

What is lost in accuracy in this drawing is gained in expression. The less precise lines of the woman in the drawing on the lower right are more lively and loopy than the lines of the woman in the mirror on the upper left. As they move away from precise description of shapes, lines can become more interesting in themselves.

**The Rock Near Montmajour,** Vincent van Gogh, Sunday, July 8, 1888
Pencil, pen, reed pen, brown and black ink on Whatman paper, 19 1/4" x 23 5/8"

Vincent van Gogh made this drawing with a pencil, a narrow-tip reed pen, and a broad-tip pen. The variety of marks is amazing. Some lines are as tiny as dots (the fields in the far left), and others are long and thick (the edges of the big rocks). Strong, dark lines mark the edges of things, like the outlines on the rocks or the tree trunks. Short and stubby ones grouped together suggest bunches of leaves or grass. Other lines, especially the crisscrosses on the rocks, create soft shadows. Because all the lines look like they were made quickly, the drawing seems to crackle with energy.

You can feel the energy of the lines better by turning this book upside down. That way it becomes harder to identify shapes like the trees, the path, or the rocks, and you can experience the lines as just lines. Try it.

Your mind always influences what you see. If you recognize a shape immediately, you are less likely to remember to examine the line that forms it. That is why the lines are easier to see for their own sake if you turn the picture upside down. The lines are also easier to appreciate if you get really close to them.

The farther away you move from this drawing, the less obvious the lines become. Here's an experiment: Prop the book up on a table or chair with some other books and look at this picture from as far away as you can get. Your mind will blend the lines together into a complete picture of that exact place.

Van Gogh wanted you to be able to imagine the rocky landscape of Montmajour on that summer Sunday, July 8, 1888. With some lines he drew the shapes of things, such as trees and rocks. With other lines he drew their shadows and suggested how round and thick and heavy they looked or how small and far away. How does this place feel to you? Is it hot and dry? Peaceful and inviting?

# LINES THAT DESCRIBE AND EXPRESS

# LINES IN COLOR

Even in a painting with many colors, lines can be important. The most basic lines in painting are brush-strokes, the marks made by a painter's brush. Usually you can see them only from up close, but some artists used them boldly and deliberately, especially Vincent van Gogh.

Van Gogh made this portrait of his best friend, the mailman Joseph Roulin, with a brush and oil paint. Van Gogh made energetic brushstrokes in many different colors. They are easy to see, especially in the mailman's face. They flow across his forehead, spilling down his right and left cheeks until they reach his beard, where they churn and swirl like waves at the base of a waterfall. The brushstrokes create a whole person out of a storm of action and change. But in the middle of all that rushing movement, the mailman's eyes are steady and bright. His cap stays firmly on his head. What would happen to the picture if the eyes and cap also moved?

Van Gogh made these strong lines so that you would clearly realize, even at a considerable distance, that this painting is a network of brush lines on flat canvas. It is not just a representation of the postman in a room. The artist is forcing you to think about the painting in two ways at the same time — as a surface of lines and as an imaginary space.

**Portrait of Joseph Roulin,** Vincent van Gogh, 1889
Oil on canvas, 25 3/8" x 21 3/4"

The simple drawing of an ice-cream cone shows how an artist deliberately controls the visibility of individual strokes. Everything you see in the drawing started as thin lines, but by rubbing some of these lines together and laying them over one another, as in the ice cream, Wayne Thiebaud blended the colors and made individual lines disappear. In the background of the drawing Thiebaud allowed the lines to separate into spidery-thin strands in order to add texture and to create an atmosphere of shifting light. The ice-cream cone seems to be spun of tiny threads of pure color, like cotton candy.

**Ice Cream Cone,** Wayne Thiebaud, 1991
Pastels on paper, 11" x 15"

# QUIET LINES

For many centuries, artists in China, Korea, and Japan have shown deep respect for the importance and beauty of line. The same instrument, a brush with a pointed tip dipped in ink, was used in these countries for both writing and drawing. Frequently words and pictures were placed together on the same artwork.

This ink painting on paper was made by the Chinese artist Ni Tsan more than six hundred years ago. He used soft lines and dark touches of his brush to describe a landscape of trees, rocks, shoreline, water, and distant mountains. As with van Gogh's drawing, it may help to turn this picture upside down to get a good look at the brushstrokes. Unlike van Gogh's energetic lines, Ni Tsan's are calm and regular. Many of them, such as the short dark strokes in the mountains, go in the same direction. This regularity, and the soft outlines of the rocks and mountains, makes the painting seem quiet. Most of the red seals on the painting were not part of Ni Tsan's design. They were added by collectors who owned the painting over the centuries since it was made.

**Woods and Valleys of Mount Yü,** Ni Tsan, 1372
Hanging scroll, ink on paper, 86" x 24 1/2"

44

Ni Tsan's lines create a mood of deep stillness and loneliness. At the top, in the center, he wrote a poem suggesting that the painting was made during a get-together with friends:

*We watch the clouds and play with our brushes,*
*We drink wine and write poems.*
*The joyous feelings of this day*
*Will linger after we have parted.*

Ni Tsan's poem makes you think more about the painting. He did not include any hint of his friends in the picture because he wanted his feelings to be symbolically communicated by images from nature.

With the writing on the paper and the scene that extends into the distance, this painting is another example of a work that makes you think about it as a flat surface and an imaginary space at the same time. Chinese artists liked to play with this mental switching, just as van Gogh and Picasso did many centuries later.

# LINES FOR THEMSELVES

Lines can be so interesting and so expressive that we can enjoy looking at them for their own sake, even when they do not describe something real.

Artists had used brushstrokes for centuries, but Jackson Pollock felt that in order to free himself to become a modern artist, he would have to find a way of painting that would break these ancient habits. He wanted to release the act of painting from the conscious, decision-making mind of the artist and make it an intuitive, spontaneous act that would reveal new, unexpected experiences. Instead of drawing with his brush, he put the canvas on the floor and let the paint pour in a thin stream from a brush or stick or can while moving his arm and body. This made a network of lines that were longer, looser, and more varied than any brushstroke could be.

Pollock's new painting method was a radical change because the artist let the free-flowing gestures of his arms and hands control every detail of the painting. Pollock was determined to let the lines show exactly how they were made. He made different kinds of lines by changing the tool from which the paint dribbled or by altering the speed of his arm or the thickness of the paint. But he could not predict the exact details of each line as it hit the canvas, and he could not stop to worry about it.

Jackson Pollock's painting is quite large. If you lay down in front of it, the painting would be about three times longer than you are tall. The size is important. When you see this picture in a museum, you are encouraged to step inside its world and follow its intense emotions as though you were riding through it on a roller coaster. The lines flow across the canvas with excitement, rhythm, and freedom. The lines of paint are sometimes extremely thin, sometimes thick and heavy, and always very graceful—but they are almost never straight. They twist, swirl, curl, and vanish behind other lines that pick up the movement. No matter which line you follow with your eye, another one gets in the way and captures your attention instead. It is like a drawing of a force field of crackling power. You can't dodge through it because lines are flying in all directions.

But overall there is a pattern to it, a rhythm like music. The darkest places are spread across the painting in a regular way, about equally far apart from one another. Each heavy, dark area seems to float in a sea of brightness.

None of the many lines here look like anything you can recognize. They are all *abstract,* not the outlines of

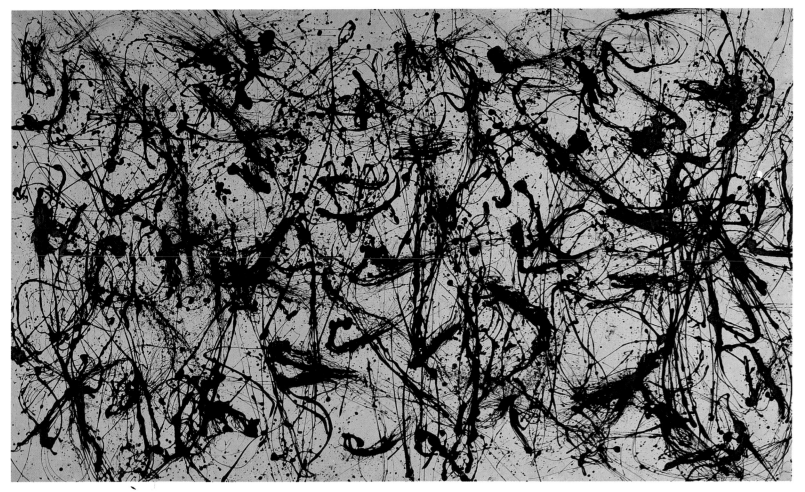

**Number 32, 1950,** Jackson Pollock, 1950
Acrylic on canvas, 103" x 177"

familiar things. Pollock is using line in the way that Kandinsky used color. His expression of energy, force, change, power, and order make no direct reference to anything specific in the real world. Do you think that a realistic picture can convey these ideas as well as an abstract painting such as this one does?

# COMPOSITION

Artists carefully position all the elements of a picture so that they can work together to influence how you look at it and how you feel about it. In many paintings and drawings, for example, the artist positions one key section or image so that it will catch your eye and draw your attention. If you keep looking at the painting, searching for clues and noticing details, you will usually discover that the painting is much more complicated than you first thought. All of its many parts work together as a team to bring you an experience or idea. This precise organization of elements is called composition.

# CENTRAL FOCUS

The first thing you notice in this painting is the boy because Francisco Goya painted his clothes in red, the strongest color on the canvas. And you are especially drawn to his large, dark eyes, which stand out in his white face. His face looks bright because it is framed by his dark hair, and the hair looks particularly dark because it is set against a bright light on the wall behind him. Using these alternating contrasts of light and dark, Goya leads us to stare at them as if at the center of a target.

**Don Manuel Osorio Manrique de Zuñiga,**
Francisco Goya, ca. 1784–92
Oil on canvas, 50" x 140"

What do you see in those eyes? Look carefully at the rest of the painting. The boy is holding a string that is tied to the leg of a bird. This is his pet bird. The bird holds a card in his beak with Goya's name on it—a very clever way to sign the painting. On the right are smaller birds in a green birdcage. On the left are three cats. All the cats are staring at the pet bird hungrily. They look as if they are getting ready to pounce on the bird. The bird doesn't seem to notice. Neither does the boy.

The composition of the painting tells you that the boy is the focus of attention, but the real excitement is the suspense on the left, where the cats are about to jump on the bird. Are the boy's look and the hungry cats related? Is the boy, innocent and unsuspecting, like the pet bird?

**The Fortune Teller,** Georges de La Tour, ca. 1632–35
Oil on canvas, 40 1/8" x 48 5/8"

# STRUCTURE

Although this painting by Georges de La Tour is called *The Fortune Teller*, it is structured around the young man near the center. He is looking skeptically toward the old lady who is telling his fortune. Two more women, one on his right and one on his left, are looking at him. At the far left a woman looks down at her hand, which is picking his pocket. The woman on the other side of him is cutting his watch chain to steal his watch. And he is completely unaware of what is happening.

To appreciate the composition here, try this experiment: Take a piece of paper and cover the lower half of the picture, everything below the young man's belt. The upper half of the painting is a fascinating arrangement of heads and glances, all very calm and very steady. Now cover the upper half of the painting, everything above this man's belt. The lower half is a complicated pattern of hands—reaching, waiting, taking, cutting. The element that ties these two parts together, the upper world of calm faces and the lower world of greedy hands, is the bright white sleeve of the woman at the left-hand edge. This two-level composition reinforces the meaning of the picture —what you think is happening may not be what is really happening.

# REPEATING FORMS

What makes a painting seem well composed? Often there is a hidden structure that ties the parts of the painting together. In order to find that structure, it helps to think of the painting as a flat arrangement of lines and shapes instead of as an imaginary space.

**Playing the Ch'in Under Pine Trees,**
Kano Motonobu, 1st half 16th century
Ink on paper, 64" x 32"

Try an experiment to discover the structure of this 450-year-old painting by the Japanese artist Kano Motonobu. Take a piece of plain white paper that is thin enough to see through when you put it on top of this picture. Tracing paper is best.

Put the paper over the picture and use a pen or pencil to draw the edge of the painting. This way, if the paper slips out of position, you can set it up properly again. Draw an approximate circle around the man playing the musical instrument (a Chinese zither, called a *ch'in*) and the man listening. Notice that the edge of the ground between them forms a line. Trace that line, connecting the two circles. Next trace the lines formed by the tree trunks and large branches. Finally, trace the lines forming the edges of the rocks.

Do you see the patterns in these lines? They fall into three major systems: (1) mostly vertical lines that point toward the musician, (2) upside-down V shapes in the center of the painting, and (3) a sideways V shape pointing to the right. These line systems organize the many details of the painting and also support the story. The vertical lines keep the focus on the musician. The lines of the trees move from right to left following the plucked notes of the music. They lead us to the listener. The third set of lines frames the space in which the music takes place. Notice the ribbons of the *ch'in* player's robes. They, too, point to the listener.

# EDGE AND COMPOSITION

By controlling how much of the subject you can see inside the frame of the work, an artist can influence the way you feel about it.

**Harriet Tubman Series No. 9,** Jacob Lawrence, 1939–40
Casein tempera on gessoed hardboard, 12" x 17 7/8"

Jacob Lawrence's painting can be confusing until you realize that it is a close-up of a heavy chain binding the ankles of three slaves, a man and two women. By arranging the picture so that it is filled with only this detail, seen from an unusual point of view, the artist concentrates on the cruelty and pain of slavery. With so little open space, the composition is heavy and oppressive. Notice the dead trees. In this depressing land the bright colors in the women's dresses are like private visions of hope. Can you imagine changing your point of view by stepping back to see what the man and women look like?

This is one of a set of thirty-one paintings by Lawrence that tell the story of Harriet Tubman. Harriet Tubman (ca. 1820–1913) was born a slave in Maryland but escaped to freedom in Pennsylvania. Before the Civil War, she returned frequently to the South at great personal risk and rescued more than three hundred slaves.

The text that the artist chose for painting No. 9 is

*Harriet Tubman dreamt of freedom ("Arise! Flee for your life!"), and in the visions of the night she saw the horsemen coming. Beckoning hands were ever motioning her to come, and she seemed to see a line dividing the land of slavery from the land of freedom.*

Once Harriet Tubman breaks her chains and escapes, her world expands, as does the open, diagonal composition of the scene in painting No. 10. Harriet Tubman, holding a red bag with her belongings, is now just one element in a large and hostile world. Half of the painting holds dangerous trees that writhe toward her like snakes. She reaches for the other half, the sky with its polestar—the freedom star that leads to the North.

*Harriet Tubman was between twenty and twenty-five years of age at the time of her escape. She was now alone. She turned her face toward the North, and fixing her eyes on the guiding star, she started on her long, lonely journey.*

**Harriet Tubman Series No. 10,** 1939–40
Casein tempera on gessoed hardboard, 17 7/8" x 12"

**Rooms by the Sea,** Edward Hopper, 1951, Oil on canvas, 29" x 40"

# SYMBOLIC COMPOSITION

With a blank wall as the central focus, at first glance there is almost nothing in Edward Hopper's painting. When you look at it carefully, however, you can find a message in the composition itself. Try starting out like a detective and make a list of everything that you notice in the painting. Write down even the most obvious things. Your final list should include at least ten items.

The center of this painting is a blank wall that looks white where the sun hits it and purple where it is in shadow. On the left side you can see a sitting room with a sofa, picture, and bureau. On the right side is an open door that looks out on the ocean. Did you find all these things the first time you looked?

To see how carefully Hopper put together this painting, take a piece of paper and cover over the right half of the painting. The little that we can see of the room on the left seems squeezed together. You can't tell how long the sofa is, what kind of picture is in the frame, or if anything is on the bureau. Now cover the left half. You get a pretty clear look at the ocean. In fact, the open doorway takes over about half of the right-hand side. You can see the horizon line far off in the distance.

The left side of the painting is cramped and feels squeezed, whereas the right side is open and you can see forever. The left side is about safety—a cozy living room with a sofa. Anyone knows how to relax in a place like that. But the right side is about danger and uncertainty. How could you use that door when it seems to open directly onto the ocean? There is no front step, no yard, no protection from the sea.

The composition of this painting implies a question: Which way will you go in your life? Will you take the easy, safe, but cramped doorway on the left or the risky, wide-open one on the right?